500·121
COMMERCIAL MICH. 34

SNAP SHOT™

Art Director Roger Priddy
Editor Mary Ling
Designer Claire Penny

SNAPSHOT™
is an imprint of Covent Garden Books.
95 Madison Avenue,
New York, New York 10016
Copyright © 1994 Covent Garden Books Ltd., London.

Photography copyright © 1991 Jerry Young.
Photography by Stephen Oliver, Philip Gatward,
Dave King, Peter Downs and Mike Dunning.
Thanks to The National Motor Museum, England.
2 4 6 8 10 9 7 5 3
All rights reserved.
ISBN 1-56458-549-2
Color reproduction by Colourscan
Printed in Belgium by Proost

Things On Wheels

Contents

*Mountain
bike*

Bluebird 20/21
Trains 22/23
Chopper 24/25
Race cars 26/27

Tractor 28/29
Cadillac 30/31

Where would we be without wheels?

Not very far. Before wheels were invented, walking and horsepower were the only means of transportation.

When were cars invented?

Cars were invented more than 100 years ago. Early cars look very different from the sleek cars you see today.

Which car would

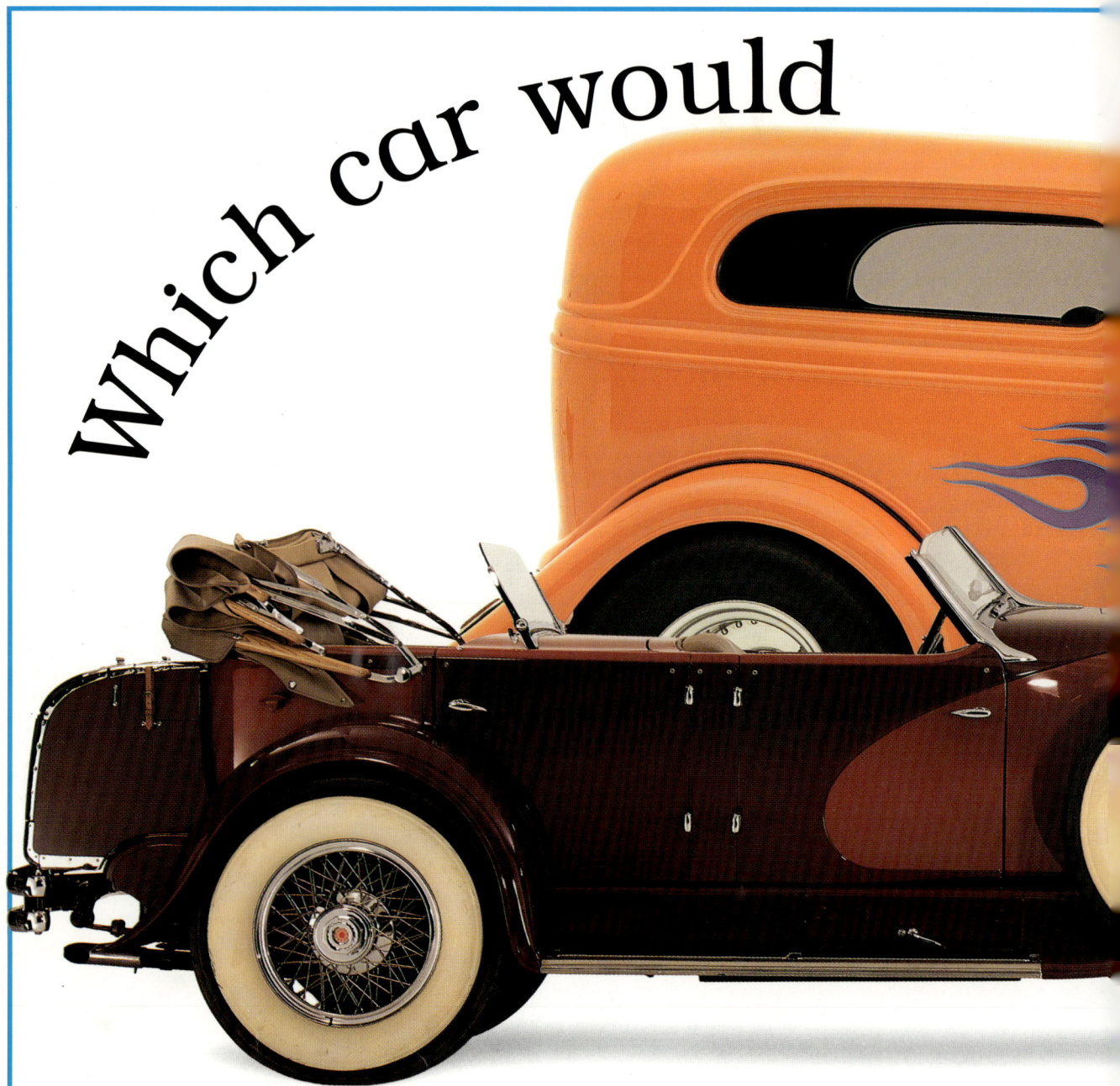

Nowadays, cars come in many shapes and sizes. Some are brightly painted,

you like to drive?

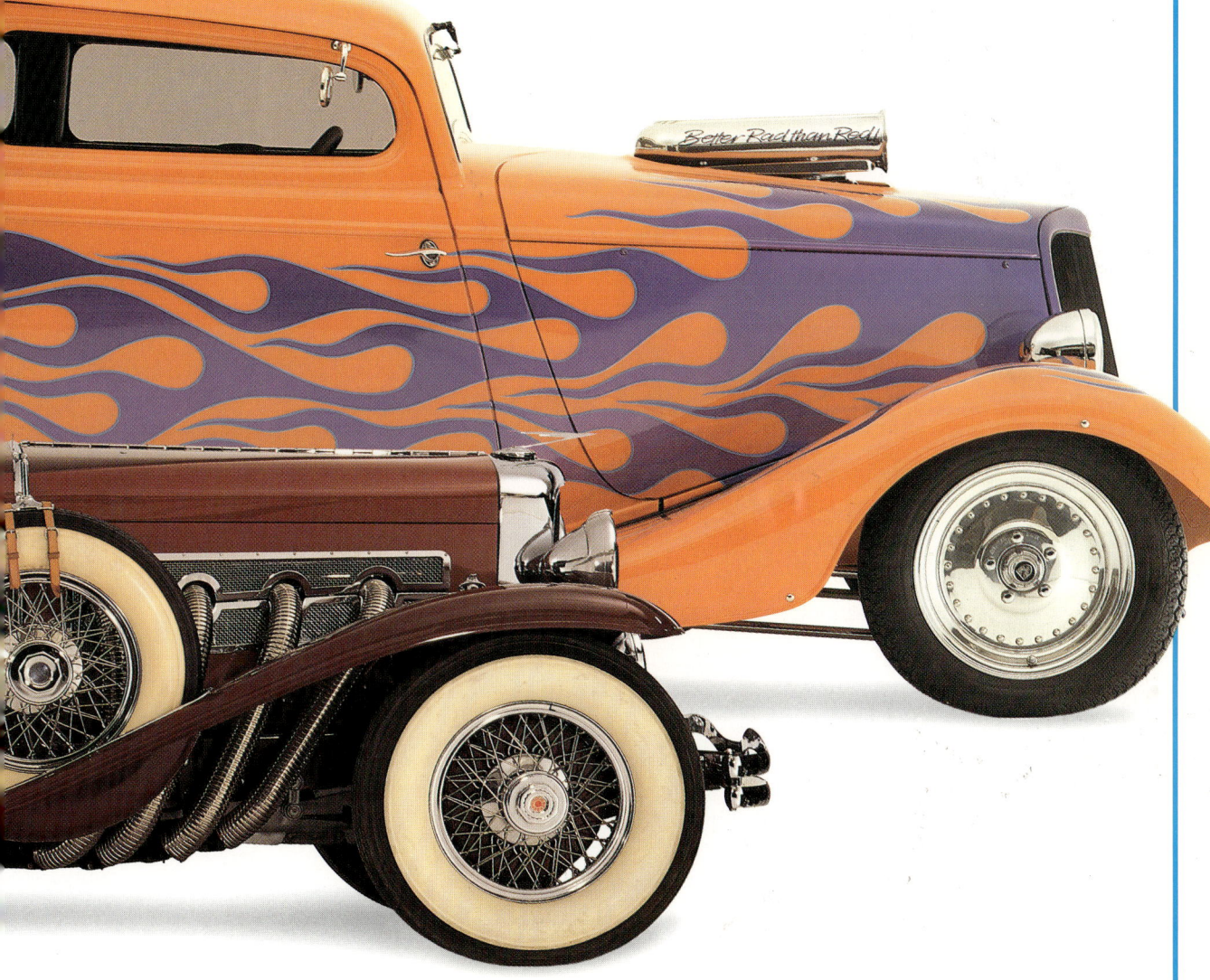

speedy, and fun to drive. Others are comfortable, expensive, and luxurious.

What do dump trucks do?

They move heavy loads,
like earth and gravel,
and then dump them
at construction sites.

What must you do

Keep your balance! Never forget to follow the rules of the road and always wear a safety helmet.

to ride a bicycle?

Bicycles were invented in Europe around 200 years ago. Some bikes are made for two or three riders.

Is this a car?

No, it's a recumbent bicycle. The rider takes it easy, lying back and peddling at the same time!

How many mirrors?

Some people like to decorate their motorbikes to make them special. This motorbike has 20 mirrors.

Four wheels or two?

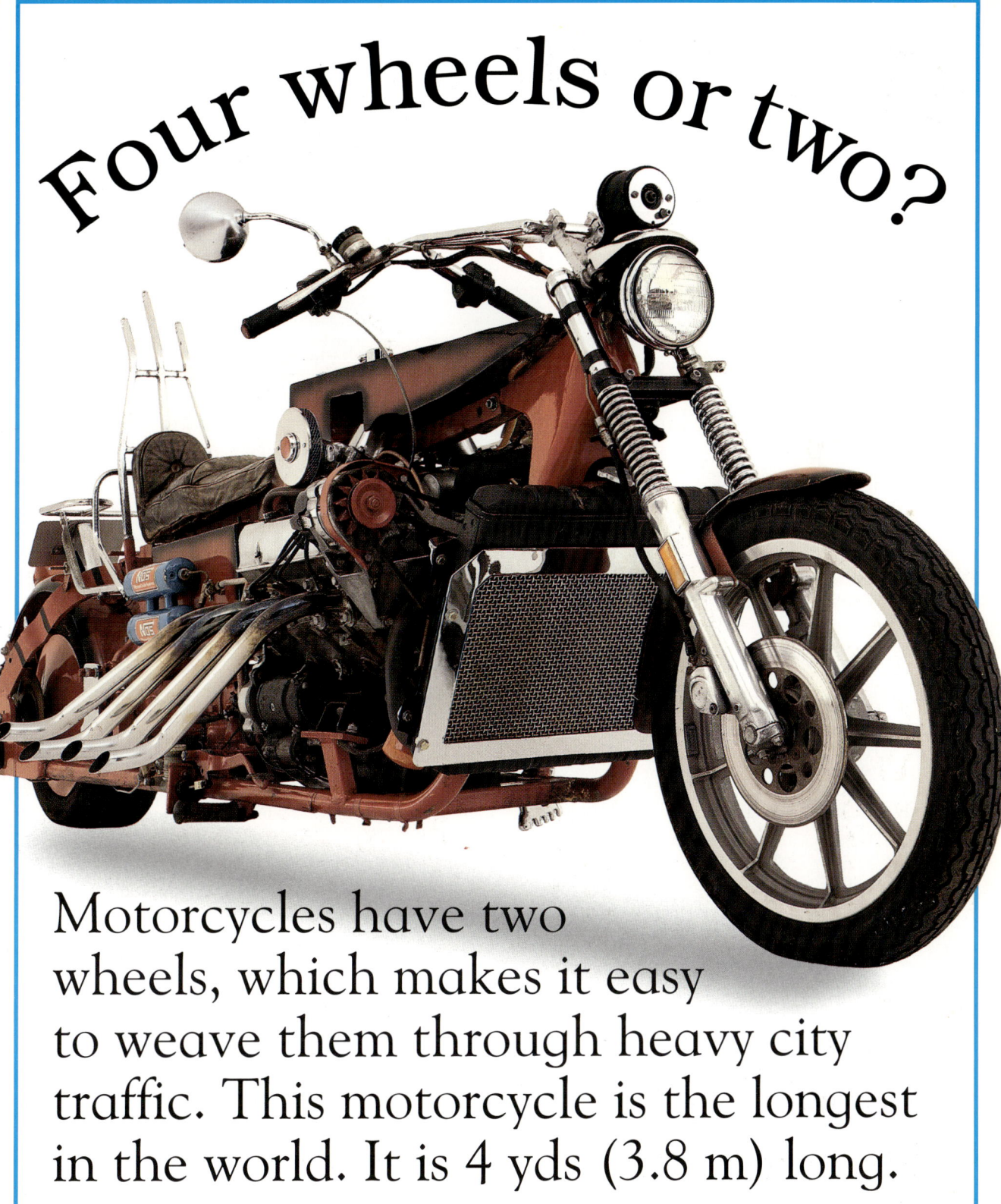

Motorcycles have two wheels, which makes it easy to weave them through heavy city traffic. This motorcycle is the longest in the world. It is 4 yds (3.8 m) long.

What is a city car?

Compacts are city cars.
This English Mini carries
four passengers, with room for luggage!

"Let's take a taxi!"

This is a London taxi.
The yellow light shows it is for hire.

How fast

This car is called the "Bluebird." Its smooth shape and fin tail helped it rocket to amazing speeds. In 1964, it zoomed to 403.1 mph (648.72 kmph), setting a land speed record.

is a Bluebird?

What do

The silver engine carries passengers on long trips in its double-decker compartments. The green engine tugs heavy loads such as coal, oil, and food in its different wagons.

these trains do?

Why is a chopper called a chopper?

People who are really motorcycle crazy "chop" bits off their bikes and add new parts. A chopper has high handlebars called apehangers!

On your mark ...

Formula 1 race cars are very
fast machines, whizzing around
tracks at over 190 mph (300 kmph).

get set ... go!

There are upside-down
wings on the back. They hold
the car down and keep it from taking off.

What does a tractor do?

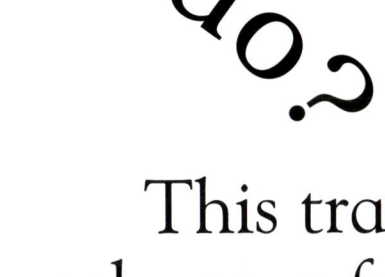

This tractor works on a farm, plowing fields and sowing seeds. It has huge wheels for crossing muddy land.

Have a

This sparkling blue Cadillac was
built especially for comfort. It is

nice drive!

a car with lots of room for passengers to enjoy a relaxing drive.